Dinner with
Catherine the Great

Dinner with

Catherine the Great

Vladimir Azarov

Library and Archives Canada Cataloguing in Publication

Azarov, Vladimir, 1935-
    Dinner with Catherine the Great / Vladimir Azarov.

Poems.
ISBN 978-1-55096-119-5

    I. Title.

PS8601.Z37D56 2012   C811'.6   C2012-901101-0

Design and Composition by Hourglass Angels~mc
Typeset in Constantia, Fairfield and Zapfino at the Moons of Jupiter Studios
Printed by Imprimerie Gauvin

Published by Exile Editions Ltd ~ www.ExileEditions.com
144483 Southgate Road 14 – GD, Holstein, Ontario, N0G 2A0
Printed and Bound in Canada in 2012

The publisher would like to acknowledge the financial support of the Canada
Council for the Arts, the Government of Canada through the Canada Book
Fund (CBF), the Ontario Arts Council, and the Ontario Media Development
Corporation, for our publishing activities.

Sales / Distribution:
Independent Publishers Group, 814 North Franklin Street,
Chicago, IL 60610   www.ipgbook.com   toll free: 1 800 888 4741

for my sister Nina

Contents

III. The Catherine Papers

Supplemental features: book-related QR codes / URLs

Scan these QR codes with your web-enabled smartphone, or access by entering the URL in your browser.

 For a five-minute video featuring the author speaking about the book, and his recitation from the poem "Catherine the Great."

Or: www.tinyurl.com/CatherineTheGreat-Azarov

 For the Author's Web site

Or: www.black-square.ca

 For a Q&A interview between Dr. Bruce Meyer, the editor of *Catherine the Great,* and Vladimir Azarov.

Or: www.tinyurl.com/Azarov-Meyer-Interview

I

A Revolutionary Night

The Boy and Future Tsar

Sun conjunct Mars in Virgo;
Mercury retrograde in Leo...
—THE ASTROLOGY OF IVAN THE TERRIBLE

under the grey sky
so dizzy high above the

earth's winter wind ruffles
a boy's fur hat with its

loose ear-flaps and
pinks his hollow cheeks

with prickly flakes
the boy's pale face looks straight

ahead with his wide open eyes
and their sharp black pupils

framed by green rims
and white eyeballs in the dark

depth of his eye sockets
young Ivan looks into the distance

firmly he stands on the
bell tower top motionless

and silent he is just seven
but he's not a child

       he is the future Tsar Ivan
       the Fourth not yet the Terrible
       he sees the mass of spinning
       snowflakes covering
       the land and
       piling up to the
       holy height of the monastery's bells
       the foggy painted landscape
       white
       the looming vague grey forest
       and the glade
       with the crooked houses

young Ivan likes this quiet
sacred place beyond his busy

court but he is not alone
the tall sheep-skinned

bearded guards look at him alertly
the brave men's

sinking hearts and shaking
hands wait for his

       Tsar's
       commands

the howling whirl drowns a
squeaky sad voice

the future Tsar asks the guards and they hand
him a bleating shivering

       white
       lamb

he takes the small gentle animal's life into
his arms kissing embracing

       then

abruptly he

              opens

his tense embrace
    above the

                 chasm

a cold indifferent obedient
           wind
           helps to
   hang
   the curling milky
   cloud

in mid-air for seconds then the
falling object dissolves

unheard invisible in the white whirl landing
without a sound a silent secret overture to Ivan's

future reign and his solemn march ahead
to the tight-fitting title of Tsar

Wandering Georgian

on her recent death,
Svetlana Alliluyeva, Stalin's daughter

Once upon a time—
She was a wandering Georgian—
                                        She was
A girl—with an impressive Southern temper

But she didn't live in her Caucasus—
Running joyfully through the mountain paths or

Wandering around the crooked streets of
The hilly Tiflis—
                        Oh no! she had a different life!

A father's only loving daughter—
                                        She saw through her
Moscow window the construction of new buildings
        Instead of the demolished churches

She watched a new enthusiasm of the new people—
She heard the grinding noise of Industrialization

The loud sounds of the discussing metal meetings of the
Strong men in the semi-military uniforms

Looking so seriously!

And the most serious of them was her
Great Father!—
God? No!
God was absent then—

She knew exactly! She thought:
"My father is a Leader! The inspirer of all our
Victories!"—
So—
She was a Wandering
Georgian in Moscow—

But she was closed in the many-roomed
Apartments with her passionate girlhood!

She thought of herself as "a bird in a gilded cage"—
Wandering around rows of rooms—
the rooms as

A labyrinth of her unsolving theorems—

Wandering—She dreamed of a freedom to wander
                              Where she wanted

She dreamed at last to run from her school
With a rucksack on her back—

But it was impossible—

                              Her girlish body
Had an inconvenient claustrophobia
        In the big car around a deep silence

Of the red-starry pistol-holding bodyguards—

                And then again—
She was wandering around the walled howling space—

From time to time she looked into the window—
And saw again Moscow's busy life—but—

        Oh but!—She thought:
"Where is the skied cupola of white or grey clouds?

Or wind? Or rain? Or storm? Or snow?
                    The free life?"

She wished
          She could touch the cold water of
The streaming river
                    Or
          Of the stormy violent ocean—

She wished
          She were on a desert island
                    (Without eyes of guards!) with
The hero Crusoe!—
          Young but bearded!

"You are a fool! Stop your imaginative wanderings!"—
                              She cried
Addressing herself.—
                    Alas—her bordered walled reclusion
Could just be stopped—in her mind—
          Or could not be stopped—
She was certain!

And in the night the crawling
Silhouettes moved on her macabre bedroom wall

Then the vague images replaced from her wall—
    Outside—

        To the Kremlin walls—and
The moving pictures unexpectedly transformed

Into the distinct real scapes—
The many many parts of the huge Earth—

The continents, the islands, countries, cities!

"My dreams are just a movie movie movie!
    Yes!
    Movie movie!" She wiped her eyes—

"Dreams will never come true for me—
        Oh! I am a hidden
Georgian girl—wandering in dreams!"—

But she dreamed so realistically and so clearly!
    So—

She was around the sacred Himalayas

Following the dead man (Oh!)
                                        Wearing white for
            His coffin
She squinted in the sunlight behind her big
            Sunglasses and

She saw through the dark-coloured lens—
The snowy bright-white shining tops—
The solemn
                        And the highest in the world—

She looked—farther—in a trembling foggy perspective
She saw the scattered ashes over the
                                    Sparkling river Ganges—

And then
            Her atheistic ritual around the sculpted stones—
She jumped, she cried, she sang,

She read poetry! But—Oh!
                                    Please stop!

The wall's silhouettes were changing quickly!
She was afraid of the nightmare!
Oh no!—

A wandering girl came to another Eden!
With dense crowds of skiing people—
It was
European Civilization
On a ski holiday!

A real dream! So nice and entertaining!
"Hey you! Wandering girl! From Georgia!

Hey! Take downhill skis for your next wandering!
Enjoy the Swiss Alps' sun! Remember your Caucasus!

Die Schweizer Alpen's Sonne!

Oh! Hey! Wake up!—It's time!"

She opened her eyes—No Himalayas!
And no Swiss Alps!—

The many lighting winking windows were
Lifting up—extending into both sides—

That was behind her own window, around her
          Red Moscow—

But she continued to dream—the tall dissolving-in-the-sky
Skyscrapers of Manhattan !

"Do you like to wander through modern architecture?
                    Known to you just from movies?
          Instead of Moscow's cupolas and spires?—

See the glass metal stone geometric prisms!—
              Or—the beginning of a New World
The shaping silhouettes of—
                    The famous—
          Frank Lloyd Wright!"—

"WHY?! WHY DO I NEED TO SEE—

                              THEM?"—
The girl from Georgia looked so surprised—

"Because this man is the most American!—Okay?"—
"OKAY"—she answers hesitantly—

Then the same inviting voice :
            "And get a guide—

American not Georgian—for your next wandering!—
Go to Wisconsin and become Ms. Lana Peters—Okay?"—

        "Okay"—
            For her it sounded so strange—

But she met an architect—the great Wright's apprentice—
William Peters! She sighs:
                "I need to stop my wandering!—
I am bent under my heavy, heavy burden!"—
Is it her voice?
            Or?
        A Caucasus mountain   faint   far away?

Mayakovsky

I like Mayakovsky on a step of cool marble
—FRANK O'HARA

Mayakovsky! I hear your voice from
my youth from my life and again... from my laptop
the small flat computer
your voice! Monumental and strong
your *Left-March*
in step... not right step... it's losing step—
just left! March! March! March! Left!

I like Mayakovsky on a step of cool marble—
Frank O'Hara loved Mayakovsky Vladimir
in Russian... Vladimir-Vladimirovich
Russian Soviet poet! American visitor!
the new world's   poetic discovery
of a full-fed
American   Life
Mayakovsky   long sailing on his ship
with   his future   futurist prospect-perspective
his personal prospect—he had an American daughter
but he was a Soviet passport holder
the Soviet poet—first Russian performer—the avant-garde artist

the art-slogan posters' creator
the PUNK verses' originator with his struggling heart
the built sculpted art figure
with his hand up! Up! Up!
toward the high restless sky with the CLOUDS!
Left! Left! Left! Left! Left! Left!

The poetic white CLOUDS—
not in the trousers... not in his hose
where the proletarian *passport* is
the CLOUDS of slogans... he cries for New Life
but Revolution   illusion   delusion
away from   the discovery of Revolution
away   from an ocean... away

from   the   sea-ship... illusion-delusion

love's   *boat crushed...*
his last poem's words of his boat of heart and of soul
his fan O'Hara seconding-echoing him decades later
I embraced a cloud—but when I soared it rained
a bitter illusion—delusion in life and in love
          mosaic as poetry
politics' illusion... his inner insight
love-feeding delusion   the lonely soul

in the tragedy
pulling his gun's trigger with the words—
　　　Lily—love me...

Lily wrote to Stalin... asking permission
to publish poetry by Mayakovsky
"the best and the most talented poet of the Soviet
epoch"—
　　　The second trigger was pulled by Stalin...
　　　O Mayakovsky! I hear your voice!

A Revolutionary Night

i)

beneath dark night
my eyes are closed—
the time is wasted
the sheets are creased
under the creaking
of my turns

my rustling howling
echo
touches a day-driven
keyboard

a quiet darkness
night blindness provokes a deep fatigue
I feel a cloudless clear changing of my mind
full of the
discovered resolutions
ahead I
cannot wait

a revolution could be
carried out tonight
in the forthcoming moment

ii)

midnight's brim
brings
a sharp tomorrow
zero hours   zero minutes
a.m.
a new morning

no bland or vapid words

before the blitzkrieg I need a rest
I close my eyes
my eyes again sleep

I need a rest
forgetting pen
still, still night
no words
the missing letters disappear
in the dismissal
and absolutely new
I am

morning rays dissolve a doubtful dark
curious sunrise   peeps at my dreams
unceremoniously
with
rude touch

the shiny
cheeky sun kisses
my lips

iii)

my lips are
closed
dawn silence honking
honking, honking
in my ears

a semi-sleeping thought
plays
a cold morning pipe
my mind's
crooked indistinct
rhythm
embryo
of a future sonnet's
interrupting rhyme

I am not
avoiding the empty void and
I am happy

iv)

the morning sun's
light
witnesses
the truth
undresses dreams and thoughts
running
away
in fright ashamed
of their night behind
the storm
in the room
a wooden ship's deck
shakes obediently
fishing my brainstorm
flashing restless prickly sparkles

my awakening
brainstorming mind
salts my motionless dry lips

v)

under the floating sky
I am curiously
watching
how
my unfinished stanza
tries to net its
snaky diving lines
for a suitable adaptation

no my allergic sea
sickness
my patient temptation is disciplined
I do not walk on
clouds I land on the soil of earth
and I am not a bird
and I am not a pilot

vi)

I do not fly
I am a land walker
I like to walk on soil
I grow with grass
I sow my simple seeds
I see my simple plants
my bloom of blue

I run around the
uneven stony rocky terraces of my last
running days
continuing my need
to play my shaman's role
my
deep infection
with a tricky shamanism

the bronze bell cries
a proof
that I am a real shaman

what is the great everlasting
art?
who knows?

Pithia says art is what lives forever

vii)

who invents
that shining
alchemic magic
stone
that transforms
a portrait of a
Florentine silk merchant's wife
named simply *Mona Lisa*
into
the Louvre's cryptic
Giaconda?

what is art?

viii)

what is art?

the lettered words
are ready to explode but try
to wait

surviving
in the hard suspense
to verse an imitation of
Petrarch's sonnet

about gentle sighs under the
quiet starry night

Insomnia

(My free translation of Pushkin's poem)

I can't sleep, the lamp is burned out;
My insomnia—it's all about—

The clock ticking penetrates—
For its end my ear waits,

The old wives babble of Fate
The trembling night is growing late;

The mice's fussing can be heard
Small but seething many words;

Do not whisper, do not blame,
Don't murmur of my lost days,

Don't light a lethargic flame—
For your boring wordless praise.

Tell me what you want, my friend,
I'm confused, don't understand,

My insomnia—my end.

Sunbeam

(My childhood's double sonnet)

i)

I am a boy—a winter window
With sunny crisp frost—morning
A forest of patterned ice and glass
A sunbeam peeking into the window
Tickling my still sleepy face
Smiling elbowing inside making room
The wet sill lets weak frost in
The morning sun bright but veiled view
Eyes hurt to look at the shining snow
No class today just warm and cozy at home
Where is my sunbeam my running beam?
I turn—the shadow of frost against
The back wall plays on the carved board
Dancing winking friendly at me—a boy

ii)

I'm looking at the window   again
I drink (O) the sunny window's light
I squint—an enjoyable warmth warms
I'm glad to hug (O) this morning at home
I spin I giggle quietly (O!)   9:30
I'm sitting at the after-eating table
(tomorrow will be my serious math test
I need my usual mark—my 'excellent')
Looking at my textbook
The playful (O) beam above my head
The hanging (O) trembling shining shaft
Not disturbing warmly brushing
(O) my still uncombed dishevelled hair
(O) still creased from my night pillow

The Lenin Library in Moscow

I did not care,
reading Proust and Beckett and Eluard...
while the other burgers played football...
—STUART ROSS

I am young and stealing
along wood-panelled narrow corridors of a
smart contemporary temple
designed like Mussolini's Art-Deco
near the Kremlin
the Lenin Library of Moscow

in size it is second only
to the Library of Congress Washington D.C.
but many of the Moscow volumes were banned
closed to me and from the crowd

I brought

a

signed

sealed

printed

permit

from my official supervisors

attesting to my faith and loyalty so funny now
kid's contents like :

the sixteen books
of Freud's inventions translated decades before this severe
regime
on *Totem and Taboo*
on Sexuality
Art and Literature
where is the politics?
or the ideology?
just an intellectual   babble
babble
then:
1919 by Dos Passos?
darkly absurd Beckett?
Ionesco's comic plays?

I am young and stealing
along wood-paneled narrow corridors of a
smart contemporary temple...

Love

What is translation? On a platter
   A poet's pale and glaring head,
   A parrot's screech, a monkey's chatter
   And profanation in the end.

—Vladimir Nabokov

(after "To K" by Pushkin)

The marvellous instant I remember,
My sparkling bright-light rapid dream,
My distant memory's hot embers,
A beauty's genius extreme.

I heard your restful voice always,
I dreamed your traits, my passion madness
Within my life without grace,
Amidst my blue, my hopeless sadness.

The time raced by. The spinning whirl
Erased your features in my dream.
I was without you, my fair girl,
And your warm voice's touching stream.

Your disappearance was a jail,
My many sad-stretched boring days,
The routine route's rough ruthless trail
Of the moon-running wary rays.

You came again! My soul awoke!
You came again, my loving dream!
My blessed bliss! Your thrilling talk!
Your beauty's genius extreme!

Again my heart is gladly beating!
Again my youth revives above
The universe of our meeting!
Again for tears! For joy! For love!

II

Dinner with
Catherine the Great

A great wind is blowing...
—CATHERINE THE GREAT

By Way of an Introduction

Dinner with Catherine the Great by Vladimir Azarov is a poem in three parts about the famous Russian Empress. The author's focus, however, is not on her national achievements and her progressive reconstruction of Russia's state machine and army; not on her expansion of Russia's vast territories; nor on her international fame as an autocrat and despot, or even her work to enlighten the backward state of Russia. Ignoring these well-known facts, Azarov attempts to throw some poetic light on the origin of Catherine the Great's extraordinary personality and on her early years. In the first and second parts of the poem, he finds his poetic source in autobiographical materials written by the Empress herself – about her childhood, girlhood, and arrival in Russia while still in her youth. Although a modest Prussian princess, Sophie of Anhalt-Zerbst – the future Empress – was a proud girl from her early childhood. As a four-year-old she refused to kiss the cloak of King Frederick the Great, and she was ten when her girlish independence emerged in her encounter with the grandson of Peter the Great, her future Russian husband.

Her dramatic marriage to her mentally and physically underdeveloped husband, Peter III, hardened her previously gentle character and proved a severe test of her personality for the future. Despite European books with stereotypes of wild Russia, which she studied in Prussia before her journey, Catherine saw many positive features in her new country and its people. Her aspiration to transform Russia into a civilized European state was greeted with understanding and strong support from the royal Russian court. An abused wife, deprived of civil rights, she nevertheless becomes the Russian Tsarina.

In the third part of his poem, Azarov pays a passionate tribute to Catherine as a great Russian reformer. If Peter the Great opened a window into Europe, Catherine the Great opened wide the doors to European culture. A political genius (she was even called a "midwife" of American independence), Catherine the Great was both a despot and yet one of the most cultured women of her time. She was a poet, painter, writer, playwright, and philosopher, who maintained connections with the French thinkers of her time and many other enlighteners

In his admiration for the great performer of Russia, Vladimir Azarov follows the statement of American historian Jay Winik, who says – "If you were at a dinner party... she [Catherine the Great] might be your most fascinating dinner partner." The author's poetic imagination leads up to the appearance of his heroine, as he meditates on the inspiring architecture of St. Petersburg's Winter Palace. Then, at the dinner table, tasting the exquisite French wine, the author sits and awaits his dinner with Catherine the Great.

—CHRISTOPHER BARNES

Sophiechen Is the Russian Queen

Yet this Tsar wasn't a man, or a Romanov,
or even a Russian.

—JAY WINIK, *THE GREAT UPHEAVAL*

i)

Today is a gloomy winter day
Of 1744.
A dense darkness
Holds the low and heavy sky.
It seems the sun went away
From life for good.
The world is a huge cloud shadow—
Snow or not—
A gloomy hanging space
Pulls and pushes nature down and an
Anxiety under the skin
Forgets the light transparent air
As no one awake can see a
Sunny joyful sky.

ii)

Yes! It is a gloomy morning.
It's Moscow but not Moscow winter
Weather: not sunny   frosty   crispy
But gloomy   cloudy—
More like foggy St. Petersburg.
The Prussian Princess Sophie and
Her Swedish mother come here
To meet
A hypothetical groom   the Grand Duke
Charles-Peter.
But Moscow's sky is not friendly
In this glum morning with
Its dull light shining
Through the windows.

iii)

The rows of palace rooms are lighted
By the many crystal chandeliers
The ceiling lights brightly illumine
The twiggy-thin Sophiechen.
The mirrors   parquet floor
Reflect her twinkling dress.
"How do you do   my Figchen?"
A boy's voice behind her. She is
In fright—no ceremony about his appearance:
And leashed to him a large hairy rat—
The scared girl almost faints:
"How do you do   Grand Duke Peter?"

iv)

The mother bows and stands aside.
The boy smiles and says:
"I don't remember you as a girl.
It was a time of my distant days.
I was such a young boy but now
I am sixteen—
Ready to marry."
She: "Happy Birthday   my cousin!"
He: "May I introduce to you a general
From my tin soldiers' army?"
The smart rat looks at her—
Again Sophie almost faints.
He: "Don't worry   he is polite
Hut—I have for you a secret—"

v)

"Give me your ear."
He whispers: "I am in love."
(She thinks: "How fast he moves!")
He cries: "I am in love!"
But she doesn't want to be an empress!
That nasty Russian girl!
Sophie smiles very nervously:
"Really?"
He: "And my auntie sent her and her
Mother to Siberia."
(The girl's mind: "So many
Secrets in the court!")
The rat squeaks loudly and sharply
And pulls at the leash.

vi)

A sunbeam pierces the room's gloom
And the boy Peter goes away.
The German Princess starts her new life.
She's now named Catherine
As a Russian Orthodox.
And Peter also is converted from
His Swedish Lutheran into
The Russian church
Losing his other name Charles.
What will happen later?
Sophiechen practises speaking in Russian.
Her head is dizzy and her delight
Changes shape every few minutes
Shimmering in different colours.

vii)

Russia is beautiful. Summer
Comes. The nights are warm and pale with light
For walking in the park after
Catherine's books lit by candles.
But half-German Peter doesn't help her
To adapt and just gives her the title of "Colonel"
Of his toy army's hierarchy. However
The sniffing floor rat is a VIP officer
And Peter's three dwarf assistants who line
Up the tin soldiers are VIPs too.
Oh! The times! He's seventeen!
The Empress aunt is glad to proclaim :
"The Grand Duke is ready
for marriage!"

viii)

The years passed accompanied by a vodka smell.
The old rat yields his position to his cheeky
Young son who is even
More hairy. Catherine remains in her
Colonel's role. Her marriage to
The weak-headed teenager looms as a huge
Disaster-to-be with his rat friend to
Whom he adds barking dogs and a squealing violin
His newest passion.
Catherine closes her ears   buried in her books
Or cuddles up to the live horse galloping swiftly
Through forest distances to meet her
Friends Potemkin and Orlov.

ix)

The auntie dies—a new upheaval!
Peter is now Tsar Peter the Third!
Catherine is crowned Duchess
But with a risky life between the throne
And dungeon depending on the
Tsar's unstable temper.
At a blithe court party an intoxicated
Tsar openly insults Catherine   shouting:
"You are a German fool!"
                    And again:
"You are a German fool!"
But she is already in the centre of the Russian
Court and her courtier friends—Orlov and
Potemkin—are the only hope.

x)

Then the Tsar is arrested and dies.
Whether the thirty-three-year-old Catherine
Is involved in his death is unclear.
              September 1762.
At the Assumption Cathedral in the heart
              Of the Moscow Kremlin
              The Great Upheaval happens!

              Wearing
An ermine mantle made from four thousand skins
Bejewelled from crown
To toe she is appointed:
              "Lady Catherine
              The Second
Empress and autocrat of all Russia!"

Catherine the Little Girl

> *She was a minor German princess, Sophie of Anhalt-Zerbst.*
> —JAY WINIK, THE GREAT UPHEAVAL

i)

It was sunny that April of 1739
When Figchen's birthday took place.
She is ten. She's a big girl. She's
Already a young horsewoman
With her favourite hobby   riding
In her father's forest at Zerbst.
She rides a horse leashed to a moustached
Friendly groom. Or also she's alone—
With her loving animal
Like a small Amazon. Her girl's heart
Beats loudly—she feels the
Wild warm vibrant body
Obediently galloping into the green
Dense depths.

ii)

When she was not yet five she
Asked them to buy her costumed
Horse-dollies instead of the dressed
Fairy princesses.
The dolls are male-trousered—
And Sophie inks their porcelain
White and pink
Smooth glassy faces with turned-up
Moustaches. They crowd
Her young girl's room.
And when she had influenza—her horse girls
(Or were they stable boys?)
Would kiss her—
To take away her childish fever.

iii)

"Be quiet *ma chérie* Figchen"—
Says Mademoiselle Babette—
Her French governess friend.
"Tomorrow we will get up early
Because the sail down river to Kiel is
Quite long." The boisterous tomboy
Continues to travel post-haste
In her bed with her pillow for a horse.
The candles shake as the moon
Peeps into her room's high windows.
Nicknamed Figchen—from
Sophiechen from Sophie—the girl is
The Prussian Princess of Zerbst—the future
Legendary Russian Empress!

iv)

She stands on deck with her Babette.
The wind reminds her of riding on
A fast horse. Such a pity—no horse
No horse-coach but a ship.
Her mother—a poor but
Noble Swede—is also on the ship with
Her haunting mad dream to be more royal.
She whispers sadly:
"My ugly duckling   poor princess,"
Nervously she lists all the dukes and all the counts
Who might be looking for brides
And now might well be looking at her girl—
Her daughter. But now they are sailing
To meet Sophie's second cousin   Russian
Charles-Peter.

v)

At the castle on the rocky bluff
Royalty surprises Sophiechen:
"So fancy tall and powdered wigs!"
Her diary note: "The stinking wigs—
not even the scattering of many rose petals
would help!" Her mother whispers:
"This royal boy is Peter the Great's grandson.
He is in line for Sweden's crown."
Sophie politely: "How do you do   Charles-Peter?"
(And asks herself: "Is he not a girl?")
Chewing a sugared pretzel
Sophie watches his pale oval face
His curly hair down to his narrow shoulders.

vi)

Charles-Peter shows her the rows of
Tin soldiers standing on the marble sill
Brightly painted with knee-high boots.
The boy:
"They are watching for the enemy!"
Sophia: "They're only stupid dolls!"
Charles-Peter is upset:
With wooden sword he knocks the
Soldiers. They fly and he explodes:
"You are a nasty little girl!"
Repulsed   she responds: "But you stink!"
He proudly: "Oh yes! I've never had a bath!
I never will and no one can force me!"
Both together: "O God! We are to be married!"

vii)

In an artist's studio Sophie sits for
Her portrait to be sent
To Her Majesty Elizabeth Petrovna
To show her what a bride looks like.
(The girl's mind:
"Please—make me pretty!"
But she keeps her proud silence.)
Two noble Russians come for the portrait.
The mother worries:
During tea she drops French phrases
In her German speech: not "that is cheese"
But *"l'est du fromage."*
The oil had yet to dry but the two Russians
Rushed the portrait to the ship.

viii)

The fourth gold autumn of fallen
Leaves and restless sky:
She is fourteen. Winter and Christmas
Come. The green branchy Christmas trees
With thorns for a wreath of God
Are an old German pagan gift.
Sophie is stimulated by the aromatic
Needles. She strokes
The live sharp trembling limbs.
Her St. Petersburg cousin has the title of
Grand Duke Peter
And waits for his Tsarina auntie's
Command for a Prussian wedding.
Sophie thinks: "What about a bath?"

ix)

Making ready for her distant winter journey
Her Lutheran papa advises: "Remain a Lutheran."
She says to him: "Don't worry   I will read the Bible."
It's her last girlish farewell to Berlin.
Her wide-skied eyes look
Through the uncurtained but
Faded sweating window of her coach at a
Not yet snowy German winter.
No papa   no siblings   no Babette. But the girl
Is not entirely alone:
Her ambitious Swedish mother
Joanna Elizabeth of Holstein is there
And three running German horses.

x)

A long long way. But it's still Europe.
The cobbled not yet snowy jolting road
Spills ink on her girl's diary.
Sophiechen is hungry to seize the
Fresh cold air. She gasps off it through the slightly
Open window. She writes about flashing
Houses   woods   churches
And the already un-German people.
A snowier track runs away eastward
With crawling long nights and days.
Sophie and her *maman* lose count of the days.
The dates change from the
Gregorian to the Julian calendar.

xi)

Oh heavens! They cross into a
Mysterious land—Russia with fur-coated
Officers. The wild wide   white plains.
Mother and daughter spend bad nights
On the rest-station floors:
No hotels with comfy beds! Wretched
Food. No one with whom to speak
German or French. They see only Russian peasants.
Oh! Unexpectedly a sleigh sent by
The Empress—thanks to Her Highness!
Finally now a smooth and pleasant ride!
No spilt ink in Sophie's diary.
A squadron of officers on horseback
Gallops to meet the noble women.

xii)

The pomp   wealth   and fame begin in
St. Petersburg
Named after the apostle Peter by its great
Founder Peter the Great
On the completely frozen Neva.
Sophie was afraid to see a non-European world.
O! She has read something different:
The huge deafening Russian copper bells
Above the crosses of thousands of the
Byzantium domes   gold onion cupolas!
Hairy bearded faces and men wearing furs of
Wolf and bear! Happily she finds instead
A European city!

xiii)

O St. Petersburg! A new Rome!
Venice of the North!
The Babylon of the Russian snowy cold!
St. Petersburg is turned into a
Great Western progressive centre with
European culture and architectural style!
A new city life and morale!
No Russian language for society and court:
They speak just French or German!
Their clothing is ordered from Paris!
St. Petersburg's opera and ballet orchestras are
Rivals to the other European capitals!
Politics?
Oh, that depends on the Tsar!

Montesquieu

In my position you have to read when you want
to write and to talk when you want to read.

—CATHERINE THE GREAT

She   exclaims: *Kiss my hand and stand there!*
She   Catherine the Great—the Russian Queen
She   says to her courtier—help me with my oil painting
She   doesn't like an old man's smell especially French

She   paints her supporter Montesquieu
She   hurries to send his portrait soon
She   opens the stone box with a thinker's face
She   looks at the fine lacquered miniature

She   has a second jewel-coloured image
She   lifts to her nose—her tiny snuff-box—
She   snuffs it looking at the micro-man
She   uses the Renaissance magnifying device

She   examines thoroughly her painted object

She   says: *Give me the thin Italian brush.*

She   says: *Not this Chinese tail of a squirrel!*

She   says: *But don't kiss my hand—stand there!*

She   sinks into a cushiony rococo chair

She   opens Montesquieu's last letter

She   sighs—*Voltaire is my only friend...*

She   looks for a proper colour: *Oh! Don't kiss!*

Dinner with Catherine the Great

> *A fragile America teetered on the brink of oblivion,*
> *Russia towered as a vast imperial power, and France*
> *plunged into revolution.*
>
> —JAY WINIK, *THE GREAT UPHEAVAL*

i)

Dinner with Catherine the Great?
I slightly duck my head under the arch
Of time. It is so easy. Just duck your head to enter
Freely. Now I am in the celebrated
        Eighteenth century!
Now I am among the shady trees of a
Chilly summer garden well-groomed
Style and sculpted in front of her
Rich marbled Rastrellian baroque
Winter Palace—the Tsarina's foggy luxury
North Venice—St. Petersburg.
        I am in 1770—
A high point in the life of the
Great Empress.

ii)

I am there. I am there. I am glad I am
Not late. Catherine the Great is truly a great figure
In 1770—a mature passionate and
                    Powerful Empress!
I did not want to see her as a great grandma who
Read her infant great-
Grandchildren the fairy tales she wrote
About Russian princes such as kind Fovey
Or smart Khlor. I won't see her
Grey-haired with glasses on her German nose
Teaching her son's sons Alexander and
Constantine via her own ABC
Textbook not in German or French but
In Russian!

iii)

1770!
Not yet the time of Ural Cossak Pugachev's rebellion.
Not yet the time of France's bloody chaos and her
Six weeks of black silk mourning for the beheaded
Marie Antoinette.
Not yet is she nicknamed— "the Midwife of American
Independence" for her refusal of
George III's request to send Cossacks
To fight the rebel Americans.
    So I am happy!
I am in Russia—and my dinner will be—
With Catherine the Great!
I am happy to be seated next to Her.
    I am happy—happy!

iv)

Not for Her great galloping and loving horses—
Not for the Hermitage She built—
          Famous rival of the Louvre—
Not for Her great cavaliers and tight-panted courtiers.
Not for Her as a wolf biting new laws for
          Her Russian population.
Not for Her feudal landlord's set of laws with an inverted
          Remaking of Montesquieu's ideas.
Not for the "Tartuffe in skirt and crown"
     As Pushkin described Her
Not for Her lightning-like Enlightenment of a deep
          Religious but dark and backward Russian folk.
Not for Her belief that Her plays were much better
          Than Molière's.

v)

No!
But simply because—She is Catherine the Great!
She is next to me at Her dinner table
Under gold crystal baroque chandeliers. I raise a glass
Already but I am almost faint and
My mind is blank. A Venetian glass mirror wall
Reflects my wide open eyes
And my scared pale face.
I cannot swallow my mouthful of wine.
I try surviving and watching
Through the closely divided Dutch window:
The early northern evening on the stone-
Paved yard of the palace and the flaring torches light up
A precise architectural space.

vi)

The uniformed guards phosphorescent
Courtiers in their tight white pants
Standing on the chessboard polished land.
I look attentively at the baroque clock column
With its clock hands spinning with clockwise precision!
                    Oh my!
A sparkling flash! I start!
I see a shining vision between the smooth
Round crowns of the French garden's lindens:
An Amazon on horseback!
The tight-panted guards run swiftly and
Help Her to descend onto the lavish carpet
Leading into the palace. She walks so proudly
Towards the closely framed glass.

vii)

I feel an unbelievable great moment!
The trembling light lights Her
Queenly smiling face! The courtiers already
Enter my chandeliered seized space!
I feel Her breezy queenly fragrance! I wait for
My crucial instant!
I try to hold my insane scream!
    Oh! Stop!
What happened? I am halted abruptly!
    No Winter Palace!
    No great Queen! Only
In my mouth the sense of a French wine bouquet!
I touch my eyes—they're open.
    The dream is over!

viii)

I am exhausted. No rest for me after the night.
I see through the window of my room:
My ordinary backyard on the soil roof of
An underground parking lot with the downtown's
Thin bent birches. The early morning.
        Oh!
        Oh! What is that?
On the sidewalk coming past the garbage bins
I see an approaching figure. Dressed as a queen!
Under her hat brim a queenly smile!
From the way out of the underground car park
One after another those white tight-panted guys emerge!
        Oh my! They are courtiers!
I run to my bedroom: my bed is empty...

Afterword

I have a confession to make. This insane idea of having "Dinner with Catherine the Great" is not completely my own. I used this original wish to get closer to the highly strung Eighteenth century as a time that gave birth to the Modern world, as described in the book *The Great Upheaval* by American historian Jay Winik. The author travels with the legendary leaders of that time across an arc of revolutionary France, a young, budding Philadelphia, and a luxurious St. Petersburg. And he gives centre stage to a powerful and fascinating female leader: Catherine the Great. I am, however, far from offering a historical retrospective of this epoch. I just follow Wink amusing musing: "If you were at a dinner party, and you got the chance of being next to Washington, or Jefferson, or Hamilton, or Robespierre, or Louis XI, or Catherine, she might be your most fascinating dinner partner." My aim is just to play, through my lightly observant Parnassian vision, with that great, enlightened, but also highly controversial figure – Catherine the Great.

—V.A.

III

The Catherine Papers

Queen

i say good morning my kind queen
don't keep your silence proudly

do not be shy and call me loudly
to your meadow so cow-green

i'll watch your tempting morning bath
your leaping into sunny green grass

i'm following my pale naked queen
my peeping tom's meadow-cow sin

i'm streaming into your slim insane inside
my cow queen's researching kind mind

i'm stealing by the crooked hidden path
i'm breathing your intoxicating poison grass

are you a kind paradise or burning devil hell?
bless my debt or trust for our meadow holy cow bell

i say good morning my kind queen
soothe me if a meadow passion is not my sin

A Desk Still Life

Today is Sunday.
A sunny frost brightly lights my desk's
Still life through the wide window—
Pens, pencils, books,
The scattered papers
A laptop and a part of it
Skype!—I hear the wireless connection
Signal—my sister calls:
"Today is the day of our father's death—
Commemorate him please!
Recall him with a vodka shot!
And can you go to the church?"
"Okay! I'll go to the church
To light a taper-candle!
But late! About one p.m.—the afternoon!
I will be in the church about three pm!"

Still didn't wash and shave today.
I'm diving into my laptop
From early morning—and now
I quickly wash and shave
And drink a cup of coffee—
I'm near the subway!

Oh! there isn't my subway today!
My line is being fixed this Sunday!
I run to a distant station—it takes some time!

Taking off
My winter hat about 3 pm
I cross my face in our Orthodox way from-right-to-left
And pull the door—the church is closed!
I see the door for the church workers—

A woman cleans up after a caterer:
"Sorry Mister! It's late! No priests!"
"I need to light a candle
With a prayer for my father's rest!
Today is the day he died!"
Then I am guided by her—through the
Church coulisse and buy for a dollar
The thin taper—and in the semi-dark
Adoring brightly the church interior—
Decor and icons—
I stick the candle into a hole of a golden
Candelabrum—Oh!
Light? Matches? No light! All the wax growing
A grass of candles is put out!
I look for the guide woman—

She runs to me with the ignited candle's light!
"Thank you! It's very kind of you!"
I say
I pray—
With words as I remember!
I find my holy icon on the wall and a long list
Of Grand Duchess Olga's cadet guard!
I pray—
As I remember! More! As I remember!

My key in my home door!
It is too late to Skype my sister
And for the Russian vodka shot with
Her on our father's day!
Anyway I go to my laptop—
What happened?
I see the back of an unknown man—
He sits around my desk place!
Still life's mess is the same!—He uses
My laptop!—
"A funny new technology!"—
My father turns to me—
"It's easy for my engineering brain!
What will come later in the world?"
My father looks not bad—

He is my age—he softly smiles—
He's never changed his facial
Expression—as I remember—
"Do you like the local church?"—
His second question.
"Oh yes! It's nice! The church was built
By the Grand Duchess Olga—
The youngest sister of our Nicolas
The Second."
"Did she survive? It's good—I did not know it"—
My father shakes his head and dissipates
Into the light of
The bright vibrant screen...

Megalopolis

*Moscow shocked me in the
embracing Ring of her endless Sadovayas.*
                                                    —VLADIMIR MAYAKOVSKY

O! Moscow—the blindly running organism—
Consisting of millions of Brownian moving cells—
The millions of people elbow their way through
Tense-eyed faces amid the dense jungle
Kaleidoscopic erected structures of churches—
Tall dense buildings—shallow shorter tempers—
The former Capital of the World's Proletariat
Along the myriads of roaring steel-iron beasts—
          A new metabolism of the so-called reborn
Life with tech-pollution for food—contemporary
Moscow's giant guts the rushing digesting
Fulfilling belly with a complex historical
Background—the miraculously surviving old
Russian Cross Puppy-Head Cupola Monasteries
Mirrored in the river Moscow & headed by the
Kremlin—its well-known red brick walls & towers
O! but not many human beings guess—with an Italian
Accent—the Roman Verona Padua
Brick walls—then the Italian creators' names
In the slim white stone cathedrals of Moscow's Kremlin

O! but the Russian sunny nature's sublimation—
In the Red Square—the festive coloured many-topped
Church of the Blessed Basil—built by Ivan the Terrible
Who blinded two of Basil's architects—
They were Russians—do not repeat the same—
O! the Seven Moscow Hills like in Pagan Rome
Or in Christ's cradle—Jerusalem—signed by
Seven Stalin Gothic-style high-rises—dominate above
The ingesting boiling organism—a new urban
Space with dazzling bright night lights—

      With a hint of the old Klondike wild West lifestyle—
      O! the extremely expensive stores of European
            companies
      The chic aristocratic restaurants with exotic food
      But shaggy stray dogs walk here always
      O! the rapidly renewed old Russian Orthodox & the
Former Antichrists (the past Atheist Communists)
Holding the thin wax church candles in the old
Restored cathedrals—oh yes! such is the running peristalsis
Of the new Russian abdomen—of the eternal Moscow—
Close to 1000 years old—we'd like to ask
Paraphrasing the words of the famous Russian writer Gogol—

      Where do you run fly rush—O Moscow? just as the
      Writer 150 years ago—we do not hear the answer

Orpheus

The night threw a blanket of dusk...
—ALEXANDER PUSHKIN

Pyotr Tchaikovsky said—"I grew up in
a quiet spot—was saturated from earliest
childhood with the beauty of Russian song
I am a Russian through and through!"

the music of the soul—Orpheus's lyre
a love lyric lyricism of Russian nature
pours the folk melodies—birds' songs—
beasts' dances—O! lute lyre string music

a piano's vibrant voice calls us in the
meadow of a fresh *Barcarolle June*—or in
a frosty *January Fireside* or *a Mardi Gras'
Winter Carnival*—O! his—*Seasons*

an Ancient-Greek—the Russian Orpheus
brings joy for our children to dance with
a kind *Nutcracker* whose cheerful nut-
cracking cracks *Christmas* nuts for kids

Orpheus's earth—*March—Song of the Lark*
April's Snowdrops—May's Starlit-Nights
July—the *Reaper* sings about *Harvest*
November—Orpheus's lyre-*troika* speeds

to reach a *Christmas-tree's X-Mas*
again it's time—for the white-green waltz
Waltz of the Flowers we bring Orpheus
distracting him from his sad *6th Symphony*

It Is the Night!

It is the night!
No! It is the day—logically—
The dark-blue starry sky—
The sun pours beams so light
The moon dissolves the stars
The sun warms clouds
I open my eyes
I cannot see my eyes are closed
I walk and see the street
I lie on my hard narrow bed
I see a light in the blue sky
I dream the light while dreaming
I run around jumping to rhyme
I'm napping now
Or I continue to drink coffee
Before a nap but during the nap
I dream a dream—I tell the dream
Awakening with the dream
With clicking lettered keys
I dream I'm dreaming
Is it night? I see the moon
The bright light shining from the sun—
In the dream it is

Day—the sun is a full moon!
Is it day? No—It is the night
The stars are very bright creating a day
So sunny the day and so freshly
For the night
Oh! The morning!—I guess finally—
After the night—Before the day—
Sleep, nap, dream,
Fainting through another death...

Friend's Mother's Tale Decades Ago When I Was a Student

"Oh, no!—I've never written poetry—
But she—oh yes!
She was a poet of that time—She was an
Acmeist—
Probably—As I remember—
Her style and she was like—the great
Akhmatova had lines like hers!
I don't remember
Exactly—oh!—
It was the early Thirties
The short new economical return to
The old time!
Called the NEP—for a couple
Of the years—A long time ago!—
Before yours and my son's birth—
For many years
She held a book—She read read read!—
About all the
Naiads of the October Revolution—
About all the women fighting
For the Freedom—Emancipation—
Human rights and—

Grasping firmly my hand she led me
To listen to Vladimir Mayakovsky—
To the Politechnichesky
Museum—to—introduce me—to HIM!
He smiled holding my
Hand gently—after her strong hot hand—and—
HE!—Mayakovsky—
He was so blindly handsome—
A loud tall performer—
With a Soviet passport in his trousers!
His voice pierced through—and—
I was a very pretty girl
Of that time's style—Short hair—
Short skirt and low belt
A long cigarette in my long fingers—
The rings of smoke—

'No Mayakovsky!'—she said powerfully!—

'You are so sweet'—she said softly—
'So sweet like these sweet candies!—
From this sweet smelling chocolate box
Of Menier—
Two chocolate candies please!—
Eat this—please—'
The second—'Mine!' she said—

'At last we have an equal and sweet
Passion—called Chocolate!'
She said to me—

Yes—I was happy—
The chocolate was so sweet
And aromatic—
The poetry whirled a romantic waltz in my
Young head but
A gramophone played an active foxtrot—
We danced without shoes
And on a sofa we drank a cognac—
Also French
She brought it also—

Oh!—sorry!—Vladimir—tea is ready—
And—
My nut pie is still warm on our table—please!
We won't wait for my prodigal son—
And your inexact friend—
Okay?"

'Twas Under Time Decades Ago

...and let them all that do thy servant hurt be ashamed.
—OLD TESTAMENT. THE PRAYER OF AZARIAH. CHAPTER 1

'Twas in a time decades ago
What is the origin of our name?—
'Twas a small boy's question and a
Boy's father said:

"'Twas a King Azariah of Judah
From our Bible—Azariah and
'Twas Zahariah in the Old or
New Testament"—of the father's memory
From the parish-secondary school
Of the village near the town of Tula
'Twas his Russian village student memory
About the King Azariah of Judah

'Twas a memory of a time that was
An absolutely different time:
"Twas no God for all of us in that time!"—
The lady teacher many times
Repeated—"No God! No God!"
No God barked   Pavlov's many dogs

With a dropping appetite
Saliva from their talking mouths

"But Pavlov was religious"—
A boy said in the class

'Twas a lady teacher's question:
"Who told you? Was it your father?
Where is he now? Ah-h-h!"

'Twas a different time
A time of the closed churches
'Twas the closed mouths

God is dead! but not through the
Zarathustrian prediction
of the Recurrence of the Pagan time—
but simply for the Orthodox World!

Boy thinks again—
How did his name come to him
From the Bible?
No father by him now to explain
The boy's name? From the Bible?
From his father's father's father?

'Twas not from the Bible on the atheistic shelves
Several thin spines of Chekhov's
Stories and a few German Hütte
Metal dictionary volumes
From the vanished father's library—
'Twas no Bible in the broken
Churches but just the old tattered
Bible in the grandmother's trunk

And somebody could read
Under the weak electric bulb:

"and Jeroboam slept with his father
even with the Kings of Israel and
Zachariah his son reigned in his stead
in the thirty and eighth year of
Azariah king of Judah
did Zachariah the son of Jeroboam
reign over Israel in Samaria
six months and the rest
of the acts of Zachariah behold they
are written in the book
of the chronicles of the Kings of Israel
twenty and five years old was he
when he began to reign
'Twas He Azariah the King of Judah"

'Twas many hundreds of years ago
'Twas from the Holy Bible
'Twas a couple of thousand years before—

'Twas no Pavlov's dogs   no lady
Teacher in that time
'Twas the atheist new-Christian
History without the flooding Cross
Above the dragging heads
'Twas Christ with a Cross above the head!

'Twas the Cross in the world's future
'Twas decades ago

'Twas the broken Cross hung
Motionlessly silently long ago
'Twas decades—so long ago
Decades so long ago—so long ago
Long ago...
'Twas from now it was long ago!

Timothy's World

Drinking coffee at Timothy's café
Not at the Second Cup
Not at Tim Hortons but Timothy's
Every time I hear a goat bleating:

"Oh please give me a coffee just a sip
Please pour it into my mouth
A spoonful of my loving drink

And don't forget to give me sugar as
In the circus"

And I incline my cup—the drops of coffee
Drip on the rose triangle of goat's tongue
Of the goat who is not from the
Ethiopian coffee inventors' herd
Related to the Ethiopian inventor
Of Russian poetry—the great Negro poet Pushkin—

"My goat! Where are you from?"

"I am from Timothy's rich dominion"—
The goat answered—

"Yes! From Timothy! From Timothy's huge herd:
From the goats—like me, cows,
Horses, chickens, and Shepherd dogs—

Oh! Then—from Timothy's steam mill on
The harvest of his own lands
With honey and meadow beehives"

"Who is this Timothy?"
No! Stop to talk goat!—I know—who Timothy is!
He was my great-grandfather from the country side—
The Russian town of Tula   leaving for Moscow's
Awakening industrial capitalism and then

Erecting many pre-Revolutionary buildings
In the sunny city of Moscow
With his smart mind and strong hands as a contractor
        builder
And an owner of his own company—

Even the Metropol Hotel near the Kremlin was built
With his participation! Then—you know—
A chime of a very special time for all and Timothy—
1917!
The horse was killed for meat by the proletariat!
The steam mill was broken by the same individuals!

Bees were flying blindly, loosing orientation!
Okay my dear goat!
You know this old story—

Do you want more to sip? Domestic animal?

I told the story to those who did not hear it
Drinking coffee at Timothy's café—

My Small Monster

for my small monster

My small monster!
My little one!
My rat crossed with a cat!
My sharp-toothed little mouth!

My rose thin gentle tongue!
You do not want kiss me?
With your fresh lips?—okay! Instead
Say something to me!

Or better—Sing!
In your sonorous Valkyrie voice
Sing me your German lied!
Something about

Fallen water noise
Rotating wooden wheels
And things of a short life's
Eternity!

Sing to me about the summer sun
A fairy miller-maid's

Inviting smile—O!
Sing about it—my little one—

"We see this also with the wheels
Oh, Master and Mistress
Let me continue in peace
And wander!"

My rat crossed with the cat!
My gentle tongue! Sing me a song
A melody—so beautiful and sweet
Of Schubert's!

Acknowledgements

I'd like to thank all my friends – poets, writer and critics – Christopher Barnes, Jay MillAr, Ewan Whyte, Allen Briesmaster, Beatriz Hausner, and Allen Sutterfield for reading and discussing this collection of poems, *Dinner with Catherine the Great.*

The poems "Sunbeam," "Love," "Insomnia," "Maya-kovsky," "Queen," "Megalopolis," and "Orpheus" appeared previously in *Black Square* (2009) published Probel 2000.

I am thankful to Professor Bruce Meyer, for his conception in organizing these eclectic poems into a balanced and solid book. My appreciation to Nina Callaghan for her insightful copy editing and review of the poems. My thanks to Michael Callaghan, for his editorial and artistic acumen throughout the publishing process of *Dinner with Catherine the Great.*

Vladimir Azarov

Vladimir Azarov is an architect and poet, formerly from Moscow, who lives in Toronto. His collections of poetry include *Black Square* (2009), *Of Life and Other Small Sacrifices* (2010), *Imitation* (2011), *The Kiss from Mary Pickford: Cinematic Poems* (2011), and *Voices in Dialogue: Dramatic Poems* (2011).

Photograph by Mark Tearle